Marketing Handbook for Home Health Agencies

Marketing Handbook for Home Health Agencies

Home Health Business Development Strategies

Emmanuel Anene

AuthorHouse™ LLC
1663 Liberty Drive
Bloomington, IN 47403
www.authorhouse.com
Phone: 1-800-839-8640

© 2014 Emmanuel Anene. All rights reserved.

No part of this book may be reproduced, stored in a retrieval system, or transmitted by any means without the written permission of the author.

Published by AuthorHouse   09/02/2014

ISBN: 978-1-4969-3685-1 (sc)
ISBN: 978-1-4969-3686-8 (e)

Any person depicted in stock imagery provided by Thinkstock are models, and such images are being used for illustrative purposes only.
Certain stock imagery © Thinkstock.

This book is printed on acid-free paper.

Because of the dynamic nature of the Internet, any web addresses or links contained in this book may have changed since publication and may no longer be valid. The views expressed in this work are solely those of the author and do not necessarily reflect the views of the publisher, and the publisher hereby disclaims any responsibility for them.

Acknowledgments

I wish to give special thanks to my wife of very many years Veronica Anene (my life wire) without whose support the completion of this book would have been impossible. My profound gratitude goes to her for being a great inspiration and for the enormous support she rendered during several months it took to complete this piece of work.

I owe particular gratitude and thanks to my four sons, Mr. Emmanuel Jr. Anene, Dr. Alvin Anene, Lt. Derrick Anene and Mr. Willis Anene, my grandson Jacob and granddaughters Olivia and Emily. I love all of you deeply. To Emmanuel Jr., I would like to say much thank you because of the extra time you spent editing the book and for the advice and sense of direction you provided me throughout the entire process.

I would also like to extend my thanks to the staff at Glowtorch Enterprises, Inc and Anene, Inc. for the work they do from which I was able to draw hands-on experience through observation and dialogues. Through this process I have been able to improve on my marketing and sales skills.

Above all, I thank GOD for the blessings HE continues to shower on me and my family.

From the desk of Emmanuel Anene (quotable quotes)

2010
"The principles of marketing have not changed, but the processes are in an evolving continuum."

2009
Marketing processes are constantly changing as the market itself dictates. The marketer must be abreast with the changing processes in order to be an effective marketer

2008
The complexities of the marketing processes are embedded in the product or services your company provides. To overcome these marketing challenges, the marketer or business development strategist must develop an approach unique to your industry and define and present to your target audience what sets your company aside from the rest.

1997
Marketing initiatives and the implementation of marketing plans and efforts are crucial to referral opportunities.

1996
The niche to your marketing efforts will be defined by what your company does best.

Preface

My aim of writing this book is to provide information regarding home health care marketing to home health agencies, home health care marketers and business development specialists or strategists (BDS).

I had dreamt of writing this book since 1996 when I first hired a marketer for Metro Home Health Services. I prepared course works and training manuals with which the marketer was taught because we could not find a book or training centers that catered to the training needs of home health agency marketers or business development specialists in the home health industry.

About the Author

The author is a Registered Nurse with over 37 years of nursing, nurse consulting, health care consulting, healthcare business ownership and long term care regulatory experience. The author served the city of Arlington on the hospital management board for two terms (4 years)

The author has a Master of Science degree in Labor and Industrial Relations, Bachelors of Science degree in Business Administration with concentration in Marketing and an Associate of Applied Science degree in Banking and Finance. The author has certificate in Long Term and home health administration.

Contents

Introduction 1
What is Marketing in Home Health 3
Qualities of an Effective Marketer 5
Confidence Building 6
Educating the Referral Sources 8
    Compliance with state and federal laws 8
    Clinical Staff Credentialing 9
    Performance Based Practices 9
    General Information 11
    Society Need for Home
    Health Services – Why Home Health 11
The Contact –Effective follow-up after the First Meeting 13
The Process of Communication 14
Techniques of Good Listening 18
    Key Point in Listening 18
Tips for Improving Communication with Physicians and Other Referral Sources 20
Summation of a Good Marketing Plan 23
    Agency Description 23
    Strategic Focus 24
    Objectives 24
    Goals 24
Current Situation 26
    Competitive Advantage 26

Market Research 27
    Growth Projections 27
Market Analysis 28
    Identifying Internal Strengths and Weaknesses 30
Market Strategy 31
    Retaining Referral Sources for Repeat Referrals 32
    Handling Complaints from Referral Sources to Maintain the Relationship 32
    Marketing Budget 33
    Monthly Marketing Budget 34
Action Plan and Implementation 35
The Anene Service & Care Management Circle 37

Introduction

Marketing a home health agency is not an easy task in this age of survival of the fittest. The problem is not in the ability to thread the ropes of marketing principles but in the achievement of set goals and success of the marketing efforts. This is one of the few observations I have made over the years in the home health industry. Marketing as in all other industries, more so in home health requires a carefully planned marketing plan and well envisioned marketing niche and marketing audience.

At one of my home health agencies, I made a statement during one of our usual regularly scheduled weekly action plan meetings to address the week's upcoming plans and events and each employee's goal for each week. During that meeting I stated that in any given week that there are no referrals that result in at least one admission, the marketer or business development specialist must consider that week a critical week and must therefore put an action plan in place to address the issue. I further reiterated ways to address the issue in other to erase any confusion regarding that statement.

In any home health agency an on-going referral is crucial for sustenance and survival. Survival means the ability to maintain or increase revenue that is above and beyond the cost of operating the business. During the past decade home health agencies have been forced to adapt to changes in the economy, technology, and the overall delivery of health care and services. Despite these changes, the number of home health agencies has increased though some home health agencies have closed due to lack of competitive edge or inability to meet licensure or certification requirements and/or standards.

Considering the present health care reform and home health regulations, the role of marketing representatives (Marketers or Business Development Specialists) is in questions. I believe that marketing in home health must constantly address the issues of character, approach, integrity, professionalism, and restraint with regards to fraud, abuse, misappropriation and exploitation, in order to restore integrity to the home health industry.

I recently hired a marketer. The marketer was put through training both internally (operation of the agency including policies and procedures) and externally (hands-on/field training). Four months after the individual was hired the agency was lucky to receive the first referral that actually resulted in admission and provision of care and services. From this illustration it is obvious that it is taking longer to win over referral sources and for marketing efforts to begin to yield results. This in part is due to the increased number of home health agencies. In Texas alone as at October 2009, there were over four thousand, six hundred (4,600) home health agencies that were active and in operation.

What is Marketing in Home Health

Marketing in Home Health environment is the ability of an individual or the marketer or the business development specialist to persuade or convince potential referral sources to refer patients to the agency. In home health the business development specialist or strategist is the marketer. Marketing in home health is the process or the activity or method or techniques of presenting, advertising and promoting the home health agency to referral sources.

How can this be accomplished?

The Marketer has to be knowledgeable, smart, and intelligent. The Marketer must also develop a marketing niche in form of presentation and services provided by the agency that is being marketed. The services provided by the agency must have an edge that is above and beyond that of the competition.

Creativity in planning and in presentation is crucial. The marketer must create a power statement that reflects how the referral source can benefit from the agency's services and patient care if a patient is referred to the agency. For example, it is understandable that a surgeon, who refers his patient to the agency after post surgery and post discharge from the hospital for an intermittent home health care, would like to have some relief knowing that his patient is in good hands. What can make this surgeon comfortable and give the surgeon some form of assurance to release this patient to the care of the agency is what the marketer must present during the marketing process.

The power statement must reflect:

1. Reassurances
2. Benefits in terms of safety and timely healing
3. Credibility
4. Knowledge
5. Trust
6. Accountability
7. Clarity
8. Powerful description of the agency's niche, and
9. Professionalism of the agency and agency staff

An effective power statement must have a memorable opening line. Something the marketer leaves behind for the referral source to remember the agency and the marketer by and generate interest in the mind of the referral source.

The marketer must try to understand what the referral source (physician, social worker, case manager, and discharge planner or referral coordinator) wants from the home health agency in terms of specialty and skills and attempt to match those needs based on patient care needs.

Qualities of an Effective Marketer

"Marketers are not born they are made"
Steps toward a good starting point:

1. Dress to impress. Be professional and well groomed.
2. Maintain a positive attitude. Avoid negativism. Smile, and show a positive outlook
3. Be determined and never be discouraged even when the doors are shut against you
4. Communicate effectively. Use proper grammar
5. Listen effectively and attentively. Understand that the referral source has a need to be met and try to know those needs. Ask questions when in doubt.
6. Take notes if need be. Marketers are always determined to win and gain referrals. That is simply the game.
7. Be trustworthy and stand by your promise because this may result in repeat referrals.

Confidence Building

A marketer needs to have self confidence. The confidence of a home health agency marketer comes from the confidence he/she has in the agency. The elements that a home health agency possesses that can help the marketer in marketing effectively lie on the quality of care provided by the agency, proficiency of staff, and the categories of services provided by the agency. These elements must also include what sets the agency apart from other agencies. What can and what does the agency do better than the competition.

The marketer should be knowledgeable about the home health industry and above all the potentials, abilities and capabilities of the agency he/she works for.

The referral sources would not be influenced by the marketer if the marketer lacks self confidence or lacks confidence in the agency. The marketer's confidence must be established and reaffirmed in all phases of the marketing process. The sooner the marketer establishes confidence in the referral sources the sooner the marketer begins to see results.

There are many opportunities for establishing referral source confidence. They are as follow:

1. ***Do your homework.***
    a. Research to know where the referral sources are
    b. Know your target referral sources
    c. What their specialties are and what their requirements are in order to be of good service to them.

d. If possible know them by name
   e. Research to know what they look for in a home health agency.
2. *Make the first phone call.*
   a. Introduce yourself and the agency. Be professional. Speak concisely, intelligently and knowledgeably about the purpose of your call. Make an effective use of the little time you have to get the point across. Use this opportunity to arrange an on-site visit.
3. *Arrange appointment visit.*
   a. Be sure to dress professionally.
   b. Be prepared to give a once in a life time presentation. *Every such opportunity is an opportunity to make a once in a life time presentation.* Whether the meeting is at the marketer's office or the referral source's office, time management is very important and the chance afforded must be taken advantage of towards the desired result.
   c. Remember that the opportunity is to build a memorable impression of yourself and the agency.
4. *Follow-up call or Follow-up visit.*
   a. The ground work for the opportunity to make a follow-up call or visit must be laid during the first visit or call by establishing a rapport. Be sure to maintain self confidence, as well as confidence in the agency. This is an opportunity to build on where you left off during your initial contact.
5. *Gifts as a door opener.*
   a. There is no law against gifts but there are rules governing gifts and the extent of compensation within the law. Be reasonable so that your gift of good intension and a token of appreciation are not deemed a kick back, fraud or waste.

Educating the Referral Sources

There is information most referral sources would want to ask and would like to know from the marketer about a Home Health Agency before deciding to refer patients to the agency. The marketer therefore must be equipped with the information.

Selecting the appropriate home health agency by a referral source can be beneficial to the referral source including physicians in establishing an appropriate risk management process. With the significant increase in home health providers in the nation and specifically in your region, it is critical that agencies establish credentialing process and referral sources review the agency's profile to determine the appropriate agency for their patients. The following is a broad list of documents, reports and policies that the marketer may have available to provide upon request.

Compliance with state and federal laws

1. Provide a copy of the ***current state license***
2. Provide a list of services provided and geographic areas served
3. Provide a copy of all marketing materials currently in distribution including brochures
4. Provide a copy of the most recent comprehensive survey conducted by the appropriate regulatory agency or agencies.
5. Provide a copy of the agency's ownership disclosure information.
6. Provide a list of related provider entities that the home health agency ownership controls or has any investment interest.
7. Provide a list of agency's management personnel including the name, title, date of employment, licensure (if applicable), and licensure verification (if applicable).

8. Provide current curriculum vitae(s) for the administrator and alternate and supervising nurse and alternate.
9. Provide evidence that the owner, administrator and alternate, director of nursing and alternate, and financial officer are not excluded from participation in Medicare or Medicaid programs.
10. If the agency is currently under any investigative action by any external or governmental organization, or if the agency has had any such investigation conducted within the past three (3) years, attach a brief description of the circumstances and the status of any such investigation.

Clinical Staff Credentialing

1. Provide a brief biography of each licensed professional employed or contracted with the agency. Include name, title, date of hire or contract, licensure type, education level, years of experience in specific areas of practice (e.g. hospital medical /surgical department, home health, clinic), and any special credentials obtained in current status (e.g. ICD-9-CM coding certification, wound care specialty certification).
2. Provide verification of licensure status from respective professional boards.
3. Provide evidence that clinician is not excluded from participation in Medicare or Medicaid.

Performance Based Practices

1. Provide a description of agency's on-call and after hours care procedures.
2. Provide a brief history of the agency's clinical management continuity. (e.g. include changes in DON or alternate, average

length of employment of RNs and any other pertinent information that will indicate stability in operations)
3. Provide a report of agency's Outcome Reports from Home Health Compare database.
4. Provide a brief description of the agency quality assessment and performance improvement activities for the current year, including how the findings are incorporated into practices on an ongoing basis.
5. Provide report of average number of visits per patient for patients served during the past two years.
6. Provide a report of census by physician for most recent 12 month period (do not include identifying names of clients or physicians; use identifier codes for physicians only).
7. Provide copy of agency's standardized parameters for reporting to physician.
8. Provide the following "best practice" guidelines implemented within the agency
   a. Fall Risk Assessment tool used, if specified
   b. Fall Prevention and Mitigation plan
   c. Skin Risk Assessment Screening tool used, if specified
   d. Pressure Ulcer Prevention plan
   e. Depression Screening tool
   f. Depression Mitigation plan
   g. Pain Assessment tool
   h. Pain Mitigation Plan
   i. Management of Heart Failure Guidelines, including reporting to physician
   j. Management of Oral Medication Guidelines, including reconciliation steps

General Information

1. Describe the agency's approach to marketing professional clinics, hospitals, and other post acute providers.
2. Describe the agency's coordination of care processes for working with other providers involved in the care of the patient. Refer areas of difficulty to the Director of Nursing.
3. Describe the agency's preferred method of communication with physician and other referral sources.
4. Describe the agency's mission for home health services.
5. Indicate if the agency currently uses a point-of-care system for documentation and if so, does the system offer physician portal for review / authorization of orders. Describe the system and process as best as you can and refer difficult areas to the Director of Nursing.

Society Need for Home Health Services – Why Home Health

Society has greater need for home health care now more than ever before. Statistics have shown that patients both young and old prefer to be cared for in the comfort of their homes while still able to receive the support of loved ones.

Home Health Care has been proven to be more cost effective than the care provided in institutionalized settings such as hospitals, nursing homes and assisted living facilities.

Home Health care provides skilled patient care, personal care, transportation, personal assistance and other helpful personalized services to individuals needing such help.

Services provided by home health agencies may be covered under Medicare, Medicaid, private insurance or other medical insurance. Individuals who are able to pay out of pocket can also receive care and services if they wish to receive home health services.

Some home health agencies are now diversified into several disciplines and skilled services in order to carve out a niche and have an edge over other agencies or competitors.

The Marketer must have adequate knowledge of the areas the home health agency he/she works for specializes and must sell that specialty to the referral sources.

The Contact – Effective follow-up after the First Meeting

Someone has given you a business card, either at a networking or social event, what do you do next? A business card is an invitation for future interaction, but how you treat that contact afterwards will determine how responsive they will be.

Here are some dos and don'ts for handling business cards to ensure that you strengthen that initial interaction and build the relationship properly:

DO make notes on the back of the card. Write down anything that helps you remember the event, the person and the conversation.

DO follow up with a nice email. Reflect on your meeting and a proposal to meet again

DO send your agency profile. Forward any information in form of brochure.

DO look up your new contact on their website. A few days after your follow up email, send an invitation to connect with you online. This expands the ways that you're able to stay in touch.

DO add them to your email list. With permission you may add them on your e-mail list. E-mail is an effective means of communication and should be fully utilized.

The Process of Communication

Communication enhances teamwork, creates referrals and solidifies referral basis. Developing good and effective communication skills takes practice and effort. It will increase your ability to perform your task effectively and will promote success in communicating the right and intended information. It is an important tool used to foster cooperation with co-workers and supervisors if one is to succeed in the work environment. It is also an important tool for the marketer if success is desired in his/her marketing efforts. Understanding the elements of communication helps explain what happens when an individual tries to relate or transmit an idea or information to others. The marketer must understand the following process:

SENDER: The communication process starts with the sender

MESSAGE: This is the information that the sender tries to send to others. Efforts must be made by the sender to make the message meaningful to the receiver.

ENCODING: The sender must choose a method (verbal or nonverbal) to send the message. This can make a tremendous difference in how the message is received.

MEDIUM: This is the method used to deliver a message (memo, hand delivery, postal service, fax, orally –telephone, sign, e-mail, etc.)

RECEIVER: The receiver is the person who the message is intended. The receiver must be able to attach meaning to the message for it to be effective. However, in the imperfect world we live in, several problems may occur.

*The message may not reach the receiver,

* it may reach the receiver and misinterpreted,

*may be buried under heap of papers on the receiver's desk, or

* may be forgotten if the message is oral.

DECODING: The receiver's ability to attach meaning to the message is crucial. The message may reach the receiver and the receiver reads a different meaning to the message.

FEEDBACK: The receiver must respond to the message to complete the communication process.

COMMUNICATION NETWORK: A system of communication instituted by management to avoid the confusion brought about by unregulated communication.

Formal Communication Networks: This is the system put in place by the organization, usually with the chain of command. The chain of command can mean that communication may flow in different directions: upward, downward or horizontal.

DOWNWARD: This occurs when supervisors instruct their subordinates.

UPWARD: This is when massages go from subordinates to supervisors.

HORIZONTAL: This communication takes place among peers.

<u>Informal Communication Network</u>: Method of interaction based on friendship etc.

<u>COMMUNICATION AS MEANS OF NETWORKING</u>: This is very important for any organization. Smart employees/communicators work deliberately to cultivate personal business relationships. This is *networking*. This is the process of strategically meeting people and maintaining contacts to get referral information, advice and leads.

NETWORK SOURCES include: Family members, Friends, Neighbors, Social Acquaintances, Associates, People in the same line of business, Communities, Churches, etc. **<u>NOTE</u>**: You as a marketer must VIEW EVERYONE AS A NETWORKING PROSPECT. You probably know more people with networking potential than you would believe.

The flow and exchange of information in health care and home health in particular cannot be overemphasized. The effective coordination of care and services is heavily dependent on good and effective communication. Communication methods most commonly used are verbal and written (including email). Both are the most effective means of communicating information amongst coworkers, contract staff, physicians, supervisors, patients and patient families.

Though in health care it is often said that, "IF IT IS NOT DOCUMENTED IT IS NOT DONE." In this regard, bear this saying in mind at all times, written communication takes precedence over verbal. This is not to undermine the importance of verbal communication it only means that verbal communication is an informal method of communication. To make your communication formal, legal and one of importance it has to be documented.

The care and services a health care provider renders to a patient is not complete until it is documented. Documentation must be executed on any legal paper approved by the agency. Documentation can be executed by professionals and nonprofessionals alike on the approved agency papers or forms. All documentations must be signed with the writer's title and must be dated. The marketer must provide plan of action and progress made in like manner to the supervisor.

Office staff, field staff and administrative staff must share important patient care information. There should be an effective flow of information in the right order among staff from when the patient is referred and throughout the period the patient is under the care of the agency.

Physicians, therapist and families or patient responsible parties must be adequately informed regarding important information related to the care of the patient. This must be followed with adequate and thorough documentation regarding what, when, where, and how of the communication.

Techniques of Good Listening

The marketer must develop effective and good listening skills. Effective listening opens the way for understanding. Listening is the most important part of effective communication in marketing your home health agency. The marketer who seems to know it all is probably not a good listener and a marketer who occupies the entire conversation or marketing meetings doing all the talking is probably not a good listener. The marketer must analyze and understand the following about himself/ herself:

- How well do you as a marketer listen?
- Do you allow the referral source to finish his/her statement?
- Are you patient when the referral source is trying to make a point?
- Are you relaxed and calm during a conversation?
- Do you take notes of important points stressed or underscored by the speaker?
- Do you try to understand what is important to the speaker?
- Do you request an explanation when the point being made is not clear?

Key Point in Listening

When you try to understand what is important to the speaker then and then alone can you attempt to meet their needs.

Some of the reasons Marketers loss focus and are not able to listen effectively are:

1. They are preoccupied
2. They assume to know everything
3. They take the other party for granted
4. They prejudge the other party
5. They visualize the solution before the speaker states his/her needs

Tips for Improving Communication with Physicians and Other Referral Sources

1. Understand the concept that the physician is the "gatekeeper" for all health care services and must be consulted in advance of the delivery of care in home health.
2. Review and understand order requirements and services outlined by the physician in that order .
3. Update the physician's data files to identify:
    a. Licensure verification
    b. Medicare beneficiary load
    c. Home health usage (monthly) including medical directorship positions held
    d. Patient record information request procedures
    e. Who can receive patient updated information in practice
    f. Who can relay orders in practice
    g. Care plan oversight billing practice
    h. Willingness to use electronic signature processes
    i. On call staff rotation
    j. PRN or protocol order preferences
4. Update the agency files with physician to identify for the physician the following:
    a. Agency credentials
    b. Management level personnel
    c. ICD9-CM coding specialties
    d. Experience level s of clinical and rehab team
    e. Outcome measure reports
    f. Order processes
    g. Telephone tree (agency)

i. Response to agency staff
ii. Patient update line
iii. Supervision of staff and patient care
iv. Complaints intake and investigation
h. After hours on-call procedures
5. Re-define in agency policies the required communications by state and federal regulations for the home health agencies.
a. Referral data, include <u>confirmation of diagnoses and appropriate ICD9-CM codes</u>
b. Approval for establishing the plan of care
c. Changes in patient's condition
d. New problems
e. Parameter variances
f. Additions or modifications to treatment plan
g. Non-prescription medication additions or changes (O-T-C, topical)
h. Unplanned transfer or discharge
6. Establish internal processes for receiving physician orders, communications and documentation
7. Plan a direct physician contact to review communication requirements and mutually beneficial needs for clear and concise communication.
8. Re-establish the preferred communication tree and methods with the physician or designees.
9. Review the physician communication forms to improve readability and information flow.
a. Do not ask question on physician communications!
b. Be sure agency name, address, phone number, and fax are clearly visible on all orders and communication forms.
c. Illegible signatures and titles are not acceptable

10. Provide duplicate copy forms of all physician orders and communications to assure consistency in patient records for both entities.
11. If using electronic records, establish physician portal for orders and communication updates, provide clear and concise written instructions on how to access and use, and promote use with appropriate training directly to physician and key staff.
12. Establish care coordination meeting with physician on a monthly or bi-monthly basis depending on number of active beneficiaries. The meeting shall be:
    a. conducted by a registered nurse or service care coordinator to facilitate physicians involvement
    b. Focused on medical necessity for home health services
        i. Review homebound requirement
        ii. Review diagnoses and codes
        iii. Review treatments provided
        iv. Plan discharge and after care arrangements
        v. Be prepared and concise with time!
    c. Document conference with signatures and dates of both parties
13. Schedule a nurse or well informed staff to attend patient visit to physician when warranted by the patient needs.
14. Focus marketing efforts to "care" not "goodies"!
    a. Provide resource information on subjects of interest to office staff and physician
    b. Keep the physician informed about Medicare changes
    c. Update his "fraud" alert reports
    d. "Take a break" moment with physicians and his/her staff
15. Conduct satisfaction surveys with physicians on a quarterly basis, in order to identify areas needing improvement

Summation of a Good Marketing Plan

The Executive Summary "sells" the marketing plan to readers through its clarity and brevity. The summary should present a description of the services provided, its target market, and its need within the market. The summary should also provide an overview of the main points of the plan and should emphasize an action orientation.

> ***Sample text***
>
> *This marketing plan renews our strategic focus on quality patient rehabilitation and returning the patient to his/her normal level or improved level of functioning.*
>
> *We plan patient care in a manner that will provide a quick recovery from his/her illness making it possible for the patient to return to the community in a short time.*

Our staff is trained and experienced in their various disciplines and they provide care and services that are beneficial to the patient's quick recovery.

Agency Description

Highlight the recent history and success story of the agency as well as data about the agency's size, and geographic coverage areas. Key partnerships such as contracts that impact patient care delivery and activities should be mentioned. Growth history should also be included to help clarify the marketing challenges and the direction of the agency.

Strategic Focus

While not included in all marketing plans, the Strategic Focus and Plan sets the strategic direction for the agency.

Objectives

State the objectives so as to address what the agency plans to accomplish within a given time frame in the marketing process. In developing objectives, clearly describe the baseline that will help assess where the agency is at, at that point in time and the anticipated goal the agency hopes to be at specific future time if the initiative is successful. This will be driven by the efforts of the marketer and the contributions made by the referral sources in order to meet the marketer's goals.

Identify the objectives:

- *By 2013, increase agency census by 30% and total visits by 40%*
- *By 2014, increase agency census by 45% and total visits by 55%*
- *By 2015, increase agency census by 55% and total visits by 65%*
- *By 2016, increase agency census by 75%. And total visits by 85%*

Goals

The goals section of a marketing plan sets both financial and non-financial targets. Goals should be in quantitative terms, to facilitate measurement of the agency's growth and performance.

Examples of non-financial goals:

> "It is planned that XXX home health Agency diversify its coverage areas and achieve a thirty-five (35) percent increase in patient load in the next two years."

"The growth factor for XXX home health agency is to increase the Medicare patients from 10 to 200 patients in the next two years."

Examples of a financial goal:

Note that it is specific and measurable: "It is recommended that XXX Home Health Agency increase revenues from reimbursements of $2 million in 2012 to $3.5 million in 2013."

Current Situation

Describe the current situation with your company.

Sample text:

The management team has been working on new contracts for intravenous infusion and pediatric home health services since December 2012. The first one month included research into the recruitment of qualified nurses and reimbursement modalities. The information gleaned from that research laid the foundation for the key information sort. Services started in February of 2012.
Feedback from referral intake nurse and the billing department indicated an excellent growth potential and profitability and therefore, additional referral opportunities are being sought to get both specialty areas running at full levels.

Competitive Advantage

Whereas the mission defines the scope of a business or business unit and the goals define its strategic performance dimensions, its business unit competencies determine the means for achieving success.

An example of a competitive advantage: "Emmanuel Home Health competitive advantage is its large number of satellite offices, more than double its competitors, making it more convenient for patients than any other home health agencies in the metroplex."

Market Research

Use Market Research to demonstrate the viability of your plan. Discuss the different types of research you performed to examine patient's needs and the needs of the referral sources including referring physicians. Remember that the patient is the central focus.

Growth Projections

Growth projections for service categories 2012-2014

Diagram A

	2012	2013	2014	Annual rate of change
Patients	100	150	200	%
Medicare	75	100	125	%
Medicaid	25	50	75	%
Total	100	150	200	%

Source: Transitional Home Health Care

Market Analysis

Discuss market trends that support your business, for example, political (governmental and taxation policies, changing legislation), economic (income levels, employment levels, inflation), social trends (demographics, lifestyles & cultural values), technological, and legal trends.

As always, cover the Who, What, When, Where and Why.

- Who are your competitors? Explain how they are better/worse/different than you?
- What is the market size? Quote reliable research findings. Use Charts, graphs and other tables to demonstrate your findings.
- What is your current market share? How long did it take you to reach this point? What efforts were involved in getting here, e.g. investment, recruitment, or staff development?
- What are the predicted trends for these markets?
- When have market trends changed? For example, has there been a change in the market that has prompted you to prepare this marketing plan, for new business opportunity in other counties or states, changes in government legislation, government approval, company mergers etc
- Where are these markets most concentrated? For example, if your marketing campaigns apply to specific geographical locations then expand on this point and discuss why you feel this is worth pursuing. As always, reinforce your points with research data.

- Discuss any rules, regulations, acts or restrictions that affect the industry/market sector?
- Discuss any conflicts or mutual gains between agency and other stakeholder groups?

With these points in mind, describe the target market for your services. It should be described in detail, and should outline how you came to the conclusion that this is the right market for your agency services.

1. Demographics – Specify the agency, size, location or for consumers, their income, gender, education, etc.
2. Psychographics - What values, philosophy, interests, character best describe your target groups?
3. Problems/Opportunities - Why do they need your services? What's not working or what do they want to work better?
4. Points of Contact - where can you find staff to meet the needs of the patients? What type of insurance coverage?

You should also state why this market is going to use your services and show what research has been conducted to come to this conclusion.

Identifying Internal Strengths and Weaknesses

Use this methodology to identify internal strengths and weaknesses, which usually include the following areas: (Please list) as per your agency

Market Strategy

After defining your agency and services, patients and the competition, you should have presented a clear picture of your company. The next step is to outline your marketing strategy.

This is a series of objectives to meet marketing objectives and goals as reflected in the plan. Ideally you should be able to identify one primary objective and two secondary objectives and the objectives must be measurable.

- Market Penetration strategies: If the agency is new, discuss how you plan to get noticed, gain a foothold, and establish a strong referral base.
- Market development strategies: If the goal of this marketing program is to grow the existing customer base, discuss how you will get the attention of new target segments, or land new referral sources within an existing segment.

Describe how you will use marketing strategies such as:

- Conference and trade show exposure
- Direct mail
- Email marketing
- Providing services that other agencies do not provide
- Offering free seminars to raise awareness and generate leads
- Providing services in areas that most agencies do not cover
- PR in newspapers and publications
- Print marketing
- Publishing articles on the Internet

Retaining Referral Sources for Repeat Referrals
<u>Diagram B</u>

Retention	Method
Gifts	
Thank you cards	
Lunches	

Handling Complaints from Referral Sources to Maintain the Relationship
<u>Diagram C</u>

Complaints	Methods
Listen	Listen and reassure complainant.
Improve	Initiate an action
Lessons Learned	Evaluate the current system in place
Educate	Educate staff and complainant
Follow up	Contact the complainant to ensure the event that necessitated the complaint had not recurred.

Marketing Budget

Populate this table with estimates for each marketing activity that will require funding.

<u>Diagram D</u>

Budget by Type	Jan-2013	Feb-2013	Mar-2013	Apr-2013	May-2013	Jun-2013	Jul-2013	Aug-2013	Sep-2013	Oct-2013	Nov-2013	Dec-2013	Yearly	%
Line Item Breakdown														
Advertising													0	-
Brochures													0	-
Direct Mail													0	-
Fliers													0	-
Promotions													0	-
Community Awareness													0	-
Seminars													0	-
Services													0	-
Fairs													0	-
Training													0	-
Web Site													0	-
Total Cost	0	0	0	0	0	0	0	0	0	0	0	0	0	-

Monthly Marketing Budget

Populate this table with estimates for each marketing activity

Diagram E

	Month 1	Month 2	Month 3	Month 4	Month 5	Month 6	Month 7	Month 8	Month 9	Month 10	Month 11	Month 12	Year 1	Year 2	Year 3	Year 4
Advertising:																
Medicare	-	-	-	-	-	-	-	-	-	-	-	-	-	-	-	-
Medicaid																
Insurance																
Private	-	-	-	-	-	-	-	-	-	-	-	-	-	-	-	-
Total	-	-	-	-	-	-	-	-	-	-	-	-	-	-	-	-
Community Awareness:																
Medicare	-	-	-	-	-	-	-	-	-	-	-	-	-	-	-	-
Medicaid	-	-	-	-	-	-	-	-	-	-	-	-	-	-	-	-
Insurance	-	-	-	-	-	-	-	-	-	-	-	-	-	-	-	-
Private	-	-	-	-	-	-	-	-	-	-	-	-	-	-	-	-
Brochures:																
Medicare	-	-	-	-	-	-	-	-	-	-	-	-	-	-	-	-
Medicaid	-	-	-	-	-	-	-	-	-	-	-	-	-	-	-	-
Insurance																
Private	-	-	-	-	-	-	-	-	-	-	-	-	-	-	-	-
Total	-	-	-	-	-	-	-	-	-	-	-	-	-	-	-	-
Seminars:																
Medicare	-	-	-	-	-	-	-	-	-	-	-	-	-	-	-	-
Medicaid	-	-	-	-	-	-	-	-	-	-	-	-	-	-	-	-
Insurance																
Private	-	-	-	-	-	-	-	-	-	-	-	-	-	-	-	-
Total	-	-	-	-	-	-	-	-	-	-	-	-	-	-	-	-
Total	$	$	$	$	$	$	$	$	$	$	$	$	$	$	$	$

Action Plan and Implementation

Tasks required to implement and monitor each strategy are listed in this section. With each task, the person responsible for the task and a completion target date are indicated. Having a plan of action with specific tasks ensures that the details are clear and that specific persons are accountable.

Identify the promotional and communications programs required to meet the marketing objectives. Separate these into sub-tasks and allocate them to individuals with completion dates. Include costs and indicators of achievement.

This is a more granular version of the table above. It allows you to manage the program by identifying and describing each individual action item.

Specify the person responsible for each item (if several persons are involved, delegate the responsibility to one person to improve accountability and reduce ambiguity), the priority (High, Medium, or Low), the target date (which should align with the Project Plan), resources that may be required, and any potential to achieving these action items.

Diagram F Action Plan

#	Action Item	Responsible	Priority	Target Date	Resource	Barriers
1						
2						
3						
4						
5						
6						
7						
8						
9						

The Anene Service & Care Management Circle

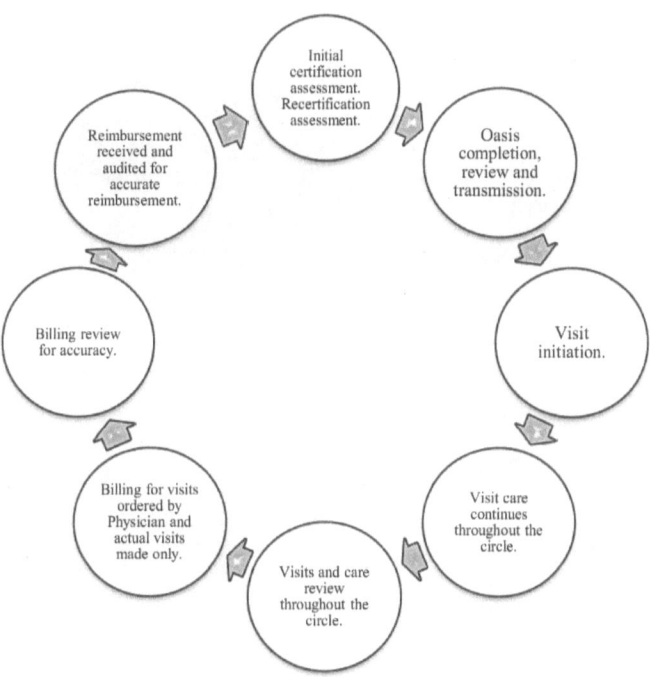

www.ingramcontent.com/pod-product-compliance
Lightning Source LLC
Chambersburg PA
CBHW021048180526
45163CB00005B/2332